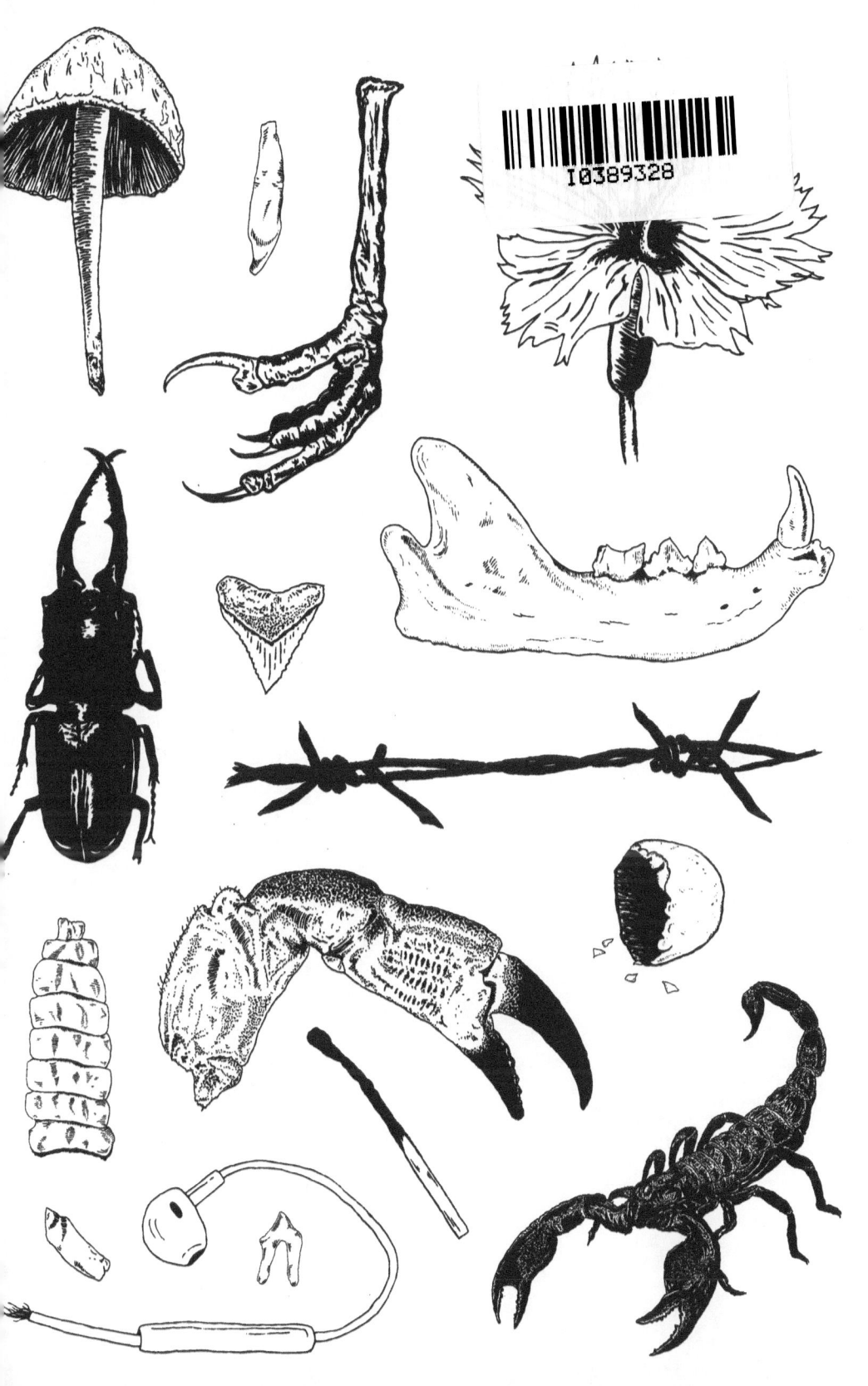

SO BELOW

LAUREN IRELAND

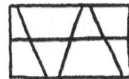

So Below ©**2021** by **Lauren Ireland**. Published in the United States by Vegetarian Alcoholic Poetry. Not one part of this work may be reproduced without expressed written consent from the author. For more information, please write to V.A. Poetry, 643 South 2nd Street, Milwaukee, WI 53204

Artwork and book design by Christopher Payne | www.saltedteeth.com

CONTENTS

RITUAL FOR BECOMING A SMALL CREATURE OF THE EVENING	5
THE BLACK BAT	6
RITUAL FOR CLEARING YOUR HEAD	9
MIDHEAVEN	10
RITUAL FOR FINDING YOUR WAY BACK TO YOUR HUSBAND	12
SOFTCORE	13
RITUAL FOR WHEN LIFE HAS FUCKED THE POEMS RIGHT OUT OF YOU	14
ANXIETY	15
RITUAL FOR RE-ENTERING YOUR OWN BODY	16
ACUPUNCTURE	18
RITUAL FOR CONTINUING TO BE A WOMAN EVEN THOUGH YOU HAVE NEVER WANTED TO BE ANYTHING LESS THAN YOU WANT TO BE A WOMAN RIGHT NOW	19
PSYCHOPOMP	21
RITUAL FOR HOSTING THE DEAD	23
ANYTHING THAT KNOWS YOUR NAME	25
RITUAL FOR SETTING YOUR WHOLE LIFE ON FIRE	27
MEMORY	28
RITUAL FOR RIDING THE SACRED DEER ACROSS THE WESTERN SKY WHILE CRYING REAL TEARS	29
ADULTHOOD	30
RITUAL FOR BECOMING UNBORN	35
I WANNA REMEMBER THINGS	36
RITUAL FOR BRINGING YOURSELF BACK	37
I THOUGHT I HEARD MY NAME	38
RITUAL FOR GIVING A FUCK	39
HOW DOES IT FEEL TO BE A SPELL?	40
RITUAL FOR BRINGING BACK THE DEAD	41
SLEEP	42
RITUAL FOR SENDING YOUR THOUGHTS ON THE WING OF NIGHT	47
WHEN THERE IS NOWHERE ELSE TO GO	48

RITUAL FOR RECREATING THE FEELING YOU HAD THE FIRST TIME YOU SAW THE OPAL FACE OF MT. RAINIER RISE ABOVE THE RAIN-WASHED CITY	51
WHAT IS THE WAY TO ANYTHING	54
RITUAL FOR FINDING AND DESTROYING THE ROOT OF YOUR MANY MANY DEEP AND UNNAMEABLE SADNESSES	55
ST. AMBIEN	59
RITUAL FOR DISCOVERING WHY YOU FEEL SO BAD	61
WINTER IS THE OLDEST SEASON	62
RITUAL FOR DISCOVERING WHETHER YOU CAN RECOVER FROM INDIFFERENCE	64
PAIN AND WONDER	66
RITUAL FOR MOURNING WHILE THE DEAD WATCH	67
THE BEGINNING OF POETRY	68
RITUAL FOR REVEALING THE SEVENTH SWORD	69
SOUNDSOUND	70
RITUAL FOR INVITING A CLOUD OF FIRE INTO A CLOSED ROOM	75
FUCKING TELL ME	76
ACKNOWLEGEMENTS	79

RITUAL FOR BECOMING A SMALL CREATURE OF THE EVENING

Let's go outside and be loud together.
Get high as ice
and watch air cleave air around your slowing hand.
When it gets dark, make a nest
of hours
and watery sun
and your hair
and the sound the night makes in your chest
and the sound of tires on wet asphalt
and your own held breath
and the feeling of waking up alone, not knowing where you are
and the time when you knew everything would be different from now on
and the last time we spoke on the phone
and
go to sleep there.
Then your heart becomes a bat
circling and circling.

THE BLACK BAT

I want to remember things
flashing like a minnow
through the brackish calm of old dreams.
That is one way for a poem to start.

When I wake up
my hands are asleep,
all my feelings left behind in a dream.
Oh I remember.
The queer pleasure of sadness, suspension
my loosened spine loose under
the anticipation of anticipation.

I remember beauty.
The startled turkey in the driveway.
Snow. The splintered icicle
in my whiskey. Night.
Winter blooms on the pane.
Rub my skin with snow
I wear away soft
under your patient thumbs.

I haven't left you.

I remember taking a bath
under the slanted ceiling
in the echoing dim, remembering
myself, knee-deep
knocking rock against rock
in Amethyst Creek.
What is inside rocks?
More rocks.

The black bat swings
from night to night,
from the rich damp dark
under the bridge
to brittle corner of day,

                    that glaze breaking
                    over browning lawns,
                       the river sleeping
                    between mossed rocks
                    the bullet-bitten signs
                       of terrible places.

            If I numbered my wet walks home
                    past the decaying porcupine
                        past the beaver-posts
                        past the sleeping-yard
                            our lost places
                 I would have a lot of nothing.

                    I am tired of getting old,

          of thinking of getting old, transparent
                    the brittle ghost with pretty eyes.
                    I'm pretty when I go back in time.
                    I love the taste of wrought iron.
                 So much more beautiful than memory.
         If forced to choose a scent, I choose cedar and wet earth.
                    If forced to choose a time, I choose not yet.

                        Even when I'm not sitting by you

                            I'm sitting by you.

                        I remember distance and thought
                            I remember all the times
                              I wished myself away
                    or on that orange-speckled girder
                            bolted to the bridge
                              the time before
                              the time before
                            the time before that.
                              Oh I remember.
                            The old boat stored
                            in the eaves, the fear,
                             gentle melancholy.

AS ABOVE   SO BELOW

You woke up so nice.

Across the bridge where love lies,
a perfect expression of desperation
like *I'm driving,* or, *I drove
over clanging bridges to find you
where you didn't want to be found.*

Where did the snow go
and who really cares?
And I woke up with all these wishes
the meteors didn't take with them.
I slept and in sleeping
knew I was not sorry.

I don't know how not to love you.
Yes this poem is about me
what the fuck else would it be about.

RITUAL FOR CLEARING YOUR HEAD

Light a cigarette on a rainy morning and let your car fill with smoke.
Exhale feathers.
If from your forehead doves pour in a mournful wonderful stream
let them feed from your mouth.
Roll down your windows.
Join the walking flock of weeping things in the wet green median.
What are all the things you have been? It doesn't matter.
The memory of the flock is short.
Worms are long. Worms are so so long.

MIDHEAVEN

Our bed is a cloud the night made
our little grey cat, its breath.
It's a night with one star
fragrant as cold roses.
Hair pins sparkle in the cracks of the floorboards.
Midheaven.
Let it fall out of you.

I can hear things in the vents
voices hoarse and sweet.
I mean
I whisper.
I want to be whispered to.

I am the thin place
where the light leaks out.
A door open wide
as a cat
for the cat-faced ghosts
to slip through
between night and almost-day.

When I am tired there is nothing
in me. All the pleasures of the senses
crushed under my dirty soles.

The pleasures of the senses
are ok with me.
You guessed it
I am awake
making a list of everything
I have wasted today.
It's almost nothing
it's like half a thing.

The window is cracked thought-wide
smaller than a thought
enough for the moon to get in.

Where are we.
When are we.
Would you unknow me if you could?
There are things I wish
I didn't know.

Peeing in the dark
elbows on knees
cold tile, excited spider
in the bathtub.
I have a secret fear
of still waters.

RITUAL FOR FINDING YOUR WAY BACK TO YOUR HUSBAND

Take off your dress
the one with the slavering wolf heads.
Let them go hungry tonight.

In the next room, your husband
is so thirsty, drinking
his own heart's blood
in warm, salty draughts.

Stand up on your hind legs.
With your sorry tongue, lick
the blood from his cheek.
Swap the heart for an orange.
He won't notice.
He didn't make your destroying sadness.

Allow yourself to soften around him.
Fold him in your hair.
Feed him your grief.
You made it yourself
with your own two paws.

SOFTCORE

Your hair is quiet to the touch.
There's a tender brown sky
and right I know
stars, wet stars
popping out out out.
The scent of approaching snow.

We want snow to change the night
and then it does
then there is
snow, weird snow
dark currents of blazing doves
fainting onto the eaves.
And I will struggle with you
in the snowstorm.

And is this weird? That I turn to you, blazing?
On fire with hieroglyphics in my mouth?
That you make all of language
into one electric verb? Yes
my name, over and over and
you are offering your mouth.

You put a hand in the ocean.
I lick the salt right off your knuckles.
I think it goes lightning, then fire.

Now it is no season.
In sleep, we are listening for its passing
the little winged moan of gone.
Things are clicking closed.
I put the moon out
I put it out.

RITUAL FOR WHEN LIFE HAS FUCKED THE POEMS RIGHT OUT OF YOU

Do not go into your terrible job today.
Sharpen all your pencils
right to the ferrule.
Remember what it smells like
to make words with your hands.
Take a nap with a live coal under your pillow.
Do not take the bus to therapy.
Paint your nails with glitter.
With each stroke, pray to your old self.
With each prayer, remember
a poem that just came out of you,
right into your little notebook.
Remember when you had long hair
long enough to knot around your fist.
Remember your special sadnesses,
your monthly bloody underwear
your poems. Your poems
your poems poems poems.
Is it ever really ok.

ANXIETY

When I walk up these stairs, I will be home.
When I turn this knob, I will be home.
I and the house will be home.
The books and the knives and the chairs will be home.
The home will be home and also all the other homes.
In all the other homes, people move through squares of yellow light.
If I am cold, the homes will huddle together to keep me warm.
They will set themselves afire to keep me warm.
I will walk blazing.
I will spark streets.
In my throat will be a hot stone.

RITUAL FOR RE-ENTERING YOUR OWN BODY

You are really far away.
You are panicked
you are eating a banana
you are forgetting your own name.

If your name is the right name
everything will be ok
in this world
and that other world
and the one where you're ok again.

You are filled with regret.
You are nausea
you are beautiful day.

Spell your name with accidents.
Spell it with little twigs or moonbeams or
pocket change or whatever.
Poetry things.

You are naive and arrogant.
You are the wig shop on 6th Avenue.
You are 6am flight to New Orleans.
You are crying a little bit.

You know what this means now
what is happening to you.
You are millions and millions of atoms.

You are in her kitchen
you are shedding her uterine lining.

Or just rename yourself
any name, anyone's name, your new name.
You can be intimate when you're dead.

You are jinx.
You are on fire.

You are feelings sweet and tender.

Or guess your own name. Name
every name, name the parts of yourself
until you are ok
ok everywhere at once and every place
in which you have ever been you and also yours.

You are like the end of a blackout
you are when all the lights come on sweetly
you are tomorrow.
You are slowly in a glittering ripple.

ACUPUNCTURE

I'm a beautiful and precious doe
grazing the low-hanging stars, etc.
Yes, there's a needle in my third eye
there's a nauseating peace
the terror of being alone
with my thoughts.

The needle in the hollow of my knee
is the needle that makes
me think of snakes
gliding across the water.
The needle in the webbing of my thumb
is the needle that
makes me want to die.
The needle in the meat of my palm
is the needle that does nothing.
The needle in the base of my throat
is the needle that sets
everything on fire.
The needle in my earlobe
is the needle that made this poem.

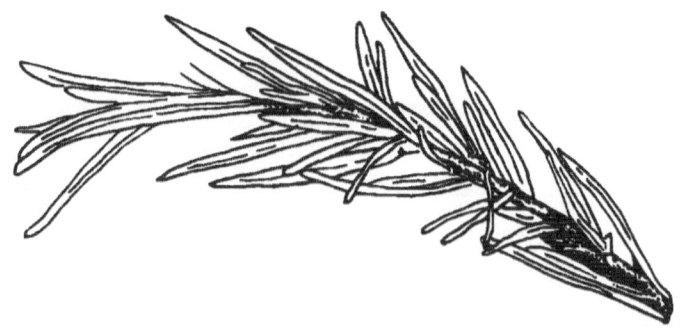

AS ABOVE   SO BELOW

RITUAL FOR CONTINUING TO BE A WOMAN EVEN THOUGH YOU HAVE NEVER WANTED TO BE ANYTHING LESS THAN YOU WANT TO BE A WOMAN RIGHT NOW

Balloon moon drifts through the doorway
bobs up to the ceiling.

Quarter the moon
quarter it again.
You have however many moons
I lost track
a fair number I guess
I don't know but it seems like a lot.

Touch each one
with that chic beige lighter.

Pop
pop pop
pop poppop pop
et cetera
however many pops it takes
to feel like you really ruined something.

Now you're in the dark.
Reach inside yourself
and root around.
Your liver is an icy opal.

Take your opal to the beach
on this new planet you have made
where it is always night.
I forgot to tell you
you have to make a planet.
Drag your fingers across wet sand,
Right across the surface of thought.

Bury your opal
deep until
all your internal light

AS ABOVE   SO BELOW

is gone
really really gone.

No I'm not happy
what do you even mean.

PSYCHOPOMP

Unfolding
over the bridge
I can see
up
my own dress.

How long
will this long sadness
lope after me
shaking the boards
collecting my nosebleeds
making nests
of my hair?

Not presence
but the absence
of absence.

All this vulvic divinity
discharge of poems
birthright of being
a lady
or whatever
I don't want it.
How many men
have chased me
away from myself?
Well
I never asked
for that.

Upside down
over the water
bats argue
about darkness
bats take
the flavor of fruit
from my very

                                            mouth.

                               Soft crescent of moon
                              softens in the current.
                                    I can only ever
                                              hide
                                inside the softness
                                       of my own
                                       soft palm.

                                       Inside out
                                  my dress drying
                                     on the rails
                        the seams like the spancel
                                       yoking me
                                         to earth.

                                    To be naked
                                         outside
                                 is to be the most
                                            dead
                             psychopomp leading
                                    my own self
                               through the trees.

                          How did we all get here.
                                   I don't know
                                    and anyway
                                        I'm not
                                         telling.

RITUAL FOR HOSTING THE DEAD

Make up a place
make it really really sacred.
Now rob it.
Take
carnelian and garnet and
quartz and steatite and
shell and carnelian and
blue glass.
Take
ways of making sure.
Take
unknown black stone.
Take
ways of making sure.
Take
carnelian and shell
and calcite and faience
and quartz and lapis lazuli
and copper and obsidian.
Take
ways past the gates
of not
being not.
Take
ring with a magical device of a bird
copper ear
sad-faced mummy.
Take
ways of being home.
Take
carnelian and shell and
faience and bone and
calcite and resin and
bone and bone and bone and
resin or amber and
garnet and limestone
and take
curls of hair at the sink.

Leave
all the ways into your own burrowing shape.
In the tomb of Perneb
I will act to your satisfaction.

ANYTHING THAT KNOWS YOUR NAME

Wash your face.
Something is crawling up the wall.
Sparks spark and
the white baboon crouches in the moon.
The bat pulls the night along.

It all feels so good.
I am an animal in your hands
wild and beating.
I flail and thump.

You walk past a noise
and now you are in the forest.
You are not in a dream.
But you are also in a dream.
Dear bats darken the water
wild and beating
I am making this path for you.

I am working on a scream
have you ever seen one?
The cry spends its whole life in my throat.

It comes fast and strange
the quick dirty scent of metal
through the air like night.
I dreamed it I swear.

Mushrooms on a wet night
anything that knows your name
edible stars
really anything could kill you.
One hand makes us
the other hand makes us disappear.

We are listening for it
the universe's hollow clangs.

        The quick dirty scent of metal
           hurtling through the night
symmetry of water deep underground.
     The moon opens like a coin purse.
                 The yells yell out.

           I am working on a scream.
              You walk past a noise.
             Metal, stone, glass, bone
          hauled across the night sky.

              We are listening for it
                 it all feels so good.
      Great frantic moons are piling up.
        Snow outside makes us feel inside.

                Do you believe me?
                Do you believe me.
            In every life it's the same
             I am savage and violent
the beetle knows my name, my name, my name.

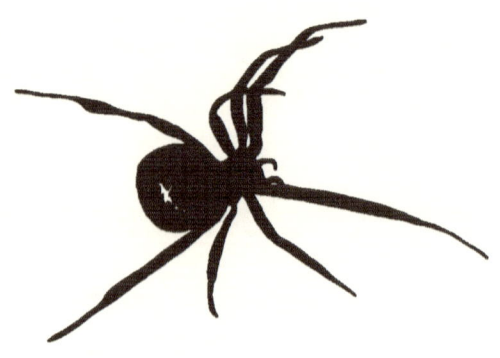

AS ABOVE   SO BELOW

RITUAL FOR SETTING YOUR WHOLE LIFE ON FIRE

Being terrible is easy.
Pour a bowl of milk
over a mountain.

Smile like the rose
the worm ate, the rose
with rain in its heart.
The rose like vanilla frosting
smeared into the soil.

Sleep is where you go to be a real person.
Force yourself to stay awake.

Now you can't even write
a poem without cheating.

Everything that is yellow has flies all over it.
Every witch is a woman
but not every woman is a witch.

As above, so what.
Is your hair long enough
is it long enough yet.

Is there metal in your pocket?
Take it out.
You are about to become
one
a witch
and two
a thing
that never stops burning.

MEMORY

I am all used up
on Champagne and bad thoughts.
Back then, when I was me
I had no fucking idea.
Now I am sad on pills
and too much noise.
It is easy to be sad here
there are so many places
for my sadness to go.

Why is beauty strange
and why in dreams
do only bad things happen?
Last night in sleep
all the wonder and all the shame.
Oh wow, I'm glowing,
sparklers alive in my guts.
I swear to god you cannot buy
this kind of shame.

I am counting down to a time
when I will be ok.

I would give you anything
to take me back
to the time before everything.
The long forever where
strange dreams, furious beauty
it all belonged to me.
I promise I will never
leave me again.

RITUAL FOR RIDING THE SACRED DEER ACROSS THE WESTERN SKY WHILE CRYING REAL TEARS

Wake up
and you are already tired.
Go to sleep tired.
Your breasts are two bruised plums
circled by a drunk wasp.
You are so close to forty.
This was never supposed to happen.

Go back to the time before "time."
Wake what's sleeping there.
Make a ladder
of your own silky child's hair.
Lick the tears
from your own smooth cheeks.
It is all very very tender.
Climb past your small curled self
curl your fingers
over the lip of the bowl
of the inverted world.

You have no idea
how far I've come
to tell you this.

ADULTHOOD

I want to be in a cold car
with all my selves
coat on
driving
in a Massachusetts I never left
or lived.
The divine sweetness of the girls
in my head
the car exhaling
dirty white
over dirty white roads.
The mountains
press the sky
press the clouds.
Far away geese are calling
I park at the party.

Cloud of golden midges
I'm in love
everything is on fire
it is four o'clock
on a Friday forever
it is almost spring
and I have never been hurt.
Sturdy yellow petals
over the turnstile
pleasure of excess
of heat
in the butterfly garden
I am already concerned
everything is past.
Nothing happens
fast enough
I will lick these peonies open myself.

Walking over the bridge of names
the darkest dark
I have ever seen

                                    dark water
                              dark cars hushing
                             over the dark street.
                         Watching the party blink on
                         sealing everything with fear.
                           Warm scent of curled hair
                           on warm dense fur collar
                          dress red as a cat's throat.
                                    Cutty Sark.
                           When we go inside the party
                                 who will we be.

                                  Loose tobacco
                                      quartz
                                faded brown rose
                              incense and silk scarves
                               at the cigarette shop.
                             Spiraling piles of books
                              under the windowsills
                                  at Troubadour,
                        names gossiping in the flyleaves
                                spiders on the porch.
                            Here is the swimming hole
                     where we prise garnets from the rocks
                          little tick sucking at my chest
                        here is where the black bear waited
                                    by the door
                           here is where we pulled over
                                      to talk
                                in the unholy church
                                 here is the shop
                          where we buy eggs and bread
                                    here it is.

                         Making faces in the convex mirror
                             I'm told this is the face
                               that makes me pretty
                              and this is the face
                              that makes me me.
                                    Wet leaf
                               on the wet skylight.

AS ABOVE   SO BELOW

                                I am the ghost
                                  at the feast
                                  I am afraid
                                of the telephone
                                     thunder
                                    the dead
                    the space between now and then.

                                The dark is alive
                             with the imagined scents
                                 of sleep and hair
                             I pull it on like a blanket
                          the night's most awful blanket
                           I'm breathing dreadful clouds
                                   like dreams
                               wet can of wet ash
                              burnt cigarette ends
                                  ice on the sill
                                  on my elbows.
                             Everyone who lived here
                                   before me
                                    is dead.
                               Is that a nice thing
                                   to tell me
                              before I go to bed?
                            Then merciful sleeping
                            into the charred morning.
                                  Honey light
                           and the frozen millstream.

                          Kitten-faced violas in a mug
                         whole afternoons on the grass
                        screen door slamming and slamming
                               fresh red blood
                                  on my palm.
                           I am thinking of something
                            tell me what I am thinking.
                                  I shouldn't
                                   but I am.

                           I don't remember anything

AS ABOVE   SO BELOW

<pre>
                    rainy afternoon on Locust
                     following smells home
                                detergent
                                  jasmine
                                    dough
                                     shit
                    the cold expensive smell
                       of the coats on the bed
                               is it wrong
                          to care about this
                                      no.

                                  Amanita
                           hen-of-the-woods
            little red one with white dots
                       every slender thing
                   that grows on the forest floor
                              has a name.
                  Brackish water has a taste
                                like fear.
                     Fear tastes like aspirin
                     inside the old cupboard
                               in the shed
                           overturned boat
                          stored in the eaves
                                    doves
                                 dove shit
                     it is not ok to be here.
                                Ferns grow
                              out of bricks.
                         The apples are going
                       with sweet dead faces.

                Wet dusty scent of storm windows
                                    ozone
            Non-shadow of blinds making vertebrae
                        watery light on the wall
        the sound of mail being sent (slide whistle of joy)
                          the dumb daily things
                  the luxury of abstinence from lipstick
                                   o world
</pre>

AS ABOVE   SO BELOW

o world when
did you get so small.

Yes
all these sounds
low and holy in my ear like night.

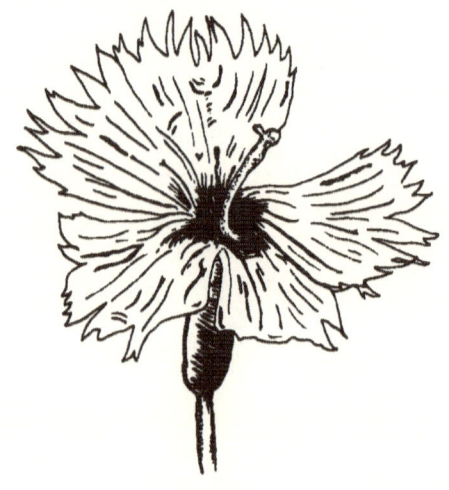

AS ABOVE SO BELOW

RITUAL FOR BECOMING UNBORN

Become a secret
that turns itself inside out
become the remotest part of yourself
become a snake that becomes a dark boat
slicing through black brackish water
rich mud, crackling dying things
quiet dead things.
The moon cuts the water and
that's where you fit your body
into the groove of cold light.
The water closes around you.
The water reflects nothing.
Think of all the things you can find
under the mud
the spinning wheel and the candle
the CD player and the candle
the teenager and the candle, where
the candle is red.
A crushed velvet something, a moon on a chain.
A crescent moon is the universal symbol for night.
A snake is a chain of memories.
Get this poem tattooed on your lower back.

I WANNA REMEMBER THINGS
I WANNA REMEMBER THINGS
I WANNA REMEMBER THINGS

I am hopeful in my bathing suit.
I learn to smoke pot
under a golf umbrella.
I have dumb memories
I bury everything
under the sidewalk's moss.
I am like to die
every time someone claps
while singing happy birthday.
If I close my eyes
No one can see me.
I am going to be pretty
enough one day I hope
I am going anywhere
other than here where
sadness grows underground
and the neighborhood sleeps
all summer and
the rusted bike chains
the chapstick the teenagers
the teenagers the teenagers

RITUAL FOR BRINGING YOURSELF BACK

Call up all your past selves.
Talk to them from your bed, your bed
in Virginia, your bed
in Massachusetts, your bed
in Pennsylvania, your bed
in New York, your bed
in California, your bed
in Washington and tell them
something spooky is happening but
you're not afraid.

Listen to yourselves breathe, and

in Virginia, the
screaming gull circling the winter beach,
in Massachusetts, the
bright tang of boxwoods in the bright air,
in Pennsylvania, the
long long night and the fear,
in New York, the
smoky October night,
in California, the
silver-rose eucalyptus branches sweeping the ground,
in Washington, the
sleeping oysters turning over
are all breathing with you.
Well maybe
actually you are a little afraid now.

Never have any of you ever been more afraid.

I THOUGHT I HEARD MY NAME

Be pretty be
the ultraviolet sibling, be
the coyote in the room, be
the fun burial ground, be
the priestess in the
zodiac bath, be
the grasping witch grass
strangling the nettle tree.

Be the only evergreen
trembling on the hillside.
Be marvelous brine, be
the burnt storm bruising the roof, be
scary magic, be
the swan skeleton in the park, be
the echoing bell.

RITUAL FOR GIVING A FUCK

Make the afternoon go away
then make it come back
different. Dark. Listen:
sound breaks
over other new sound.
Unbraid your hair
shake it loose
weave into it the ribbon of your rage.

Your home has many chambers.
let them come out of you
just like that.
Close your eyes.
Take one thousand left turns
through the spiral of yourselves.

Open your eyes.
Find your way back.
There is no back.

There are things you wish
you didn't know.

Haven't you seen other parts of being alive.
Don't you care.
And what are you thinking
and is it safe?
And where are you
and when
will you be?

Listen.
Listen.
You are the only other.
No one leaves the house and
the music is so much music.

HOW DOES IT FEEL TO BE A SPELL?

How does it feel
to be a spell?

Unborn, reddish
it's about half a thought or
like the edge of a dream
I don't know
what am I supposed to feel?

In my last three lives
I was a kitten
little sad-faced cat
slipping between worlds.

I ate a black bee
a yellow bee
a red bat
an orange bat.

I'm assuming that this
is how I died.
Little bat-faced kitten
nuzzling a ghost.

RITUAL FOR BRINGING BACK THE DEAD

Turn on all the lights.
Turn yourself inside out.
No candles.
Become your own scream.
Your saliva is turning into tears.
Your blood's salt is tears.
Turn off all the lights.
Take an Oxycodone.
Go lay down.
Your brain is awake.
Your body is asleep.
See how you are not afraid because drugs.
Wait.
Wait.
The dead will come while you don't sleep.
Now darkness turns into a shape.
Name the shape, call its name.
Is it who you wanted to see.
No.
And it's not going to be.

SLEEP

It's a dream that recurs.

Mowing the lawn at night
stars set low
driven through the heart
of the dream
the edges of the night
where rabbits gather
the edges of the night
where ghosts gather
the thing that never happened
the wonderful thing that keeps happening.

I forget the dream
that is my terrific flaw.

I'm counting
the postures of sleep.
one long shadow
two loose fists
three tangled blankets
folds the sheets leave
gently pressed into skin.

The dream-book tells me
how to be a person.

Abalone
is loneliness.

Bees
are the hum
of something approaching.

Bats
are sorrow and calamity.

Beetles

are poverty and small ills.

Cake
is despair.

A cordless phone
is despair.

Clouds
are something nice.

Dreams
are a joke.

Eggs
are secrets.

If you dream of finding something
you will wake up sad.

Fog
is obscurity or fog is clarity.

Gas stations at night
are waiting for something for a long long time.

Gates
are danger.

Ghosts
are the end of a love affair.

Green amethysts
are constancy.

Hair
is binding.

High school
is something bad about to happen.

Hotels
are between.

Ice
is a sign.

Jasmine
is bad luck.

A kitten
is small.

Knowing or unknowing
will make you equally unhappy.

Loosening
is uncertainty.

Lipstick
is someone lying to you.

A mirror
is someone watching you from a distance.

If you dream of names
you will become yourself.

If you dream of nothing
you will be lucky all your life.

October
is beauty that belongs only to you.

Opal
is change.

Poetry
is change.

Quiet
is a new season.

AS ABOVE SO BELOW

Rabbits
are a surprise.

7-11
is time travel.

Snakes
are rebirth.

Teeth
are Death's confetti.

Unborn animals
are something hidden that will be revealed.

Faraway voices
are someone lost.

Water
is a friendly ghost.

Winter
is a warning.

Worms
are a long life underground.

X
is fear, falling, fallen.

You, yourself
are asleep and
the jetty reaches
far into the night
and brings the sea.

Z is sleep
of course it is, it is
my brain sorting through the days.

AS ABOVE   SO BELOW

I think I am
retelling the dream
while I'm still in it.
I didn't mean to do that.

There is no music
I would like to hear.

RITUAL FOR SENDING YOUR THOUGHTS ON THE WING OF NIGHT

Find the negative of night.
Make an anti-sound
the sound of held breath
the sound of light
that falls and catches.
Find the kind of knowing
that tastes like ice
the fresh red of knowing
the flame
that other way in.

You aren't telling the dream
but you are there.
Ignite the long hill in a string of lights
one by one
over your shoulder
it happens
and you just know.

WHEN THERE IS NOWHERE ELSE TO GO

My heart is a hotel room
and I am alone here tonight
cold windows, cold sheets, warm breath
cold city sparkling coldly below
time drying on my thighs.
If you ask me, I will tell you:
even as a child, I knew
childhood was a mistake.

It's been a long day.

Now I am 37. The mornings go on
until four o'clock.
That is when I am closest to death.
Today I am eating tulip leaves, dying of water.
Because there is the unreal
and then there is the really really unreal.
When you are my age you will understand.

My hair grows long and I cut it
my hair grows long again and I cut it again.
Change is seduction.
Change is seduction,
seduction is a message:
you could never be this again
even if you wanted it.
Now I am 37.

Who even am I
hungover, not even real
I froze my eyes with the lip of a Coke can.
Well water and jasmine
milk milk lemonade
the perfume of the suburbs haunts my hangover
and every ex-boyfriend finds me on the internet.
I was drunk enough to look in the mirror
and think, this is ok.
Now I am stoned, eating cake in bed.

Sorrow is a long game.

When there is nowhere else to go
past all desire, past the place of feelings
my hands are sexy lions
hunting in the yellow forests of memory.
I don't want to remember things.
Paper like moth wings
those folded notes
soft foxed edges.
Handful of pony beads.
High school high school high school.
Why won't you help me not feel like this?
All the dying commas fall
blazing from the sky.

The moon has a drunken face
laughing and laughing over the gravel drive
in the blood-bright October air.
The truth is not that bad
coming from you.
But when the truth is
coming for you
that is another story.
Who can loosen a Champagne muselet with her teeth?
Uh-oh.
I can.

Are we ever not within a breath of hell?
Jim Beams, like 3 or 4 of them, and
I am past reason.
I am licking the tender inside
of my own tender elbow.
I am the rickety queen of my own bed.

The last time I was beautiful I
carried the cold in on my coat
carried a book wrapped in brown paper,
a surprise. My hair a crown of braids.
Candlelight, fat glasses of golden wine.
Be careful what you wish for

AS ABOVE　　　　　　　　　　　　　　　　　　　　　　　SO BELOW

in the airport bar.
Now I am burning
and burning in circles.
My crown is fire. No, rain. No, fire.
My crown is the heat of things passing.

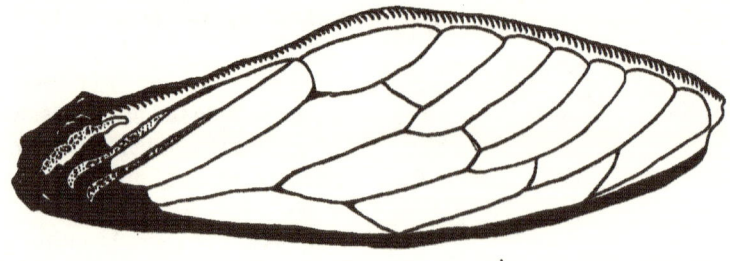

AS ABOVE SO BELOW

RITUAL FOR RECREATING THE FEELING YOU HAD THE FIRST TIME YOU SAW THE OPAL FACE OF MT. RAINIER RISE ABOVE THE RAIN-WASHED CITY

Remember the first time you saw
the Cascades on fire
with morning's cleansing light.
Peel the red bark from the madrone tree
shred the petals of a camellia.
Roll it up and smoke it.
If cold feels wet
if hot feels sharp
you're high.

What is time?

Human-headed birds
peck at coffee grounds.
Night makes dark puddles
in the kitchen. Forces of chaos
threaten the sweetly ordered universe,
the many-many helices swirling
around your many-many possible lives.

Close the window
close the window.
Close the goddamn window.

Now it is sort of raining.
Lick the scent of summer
dust from the window screen.
Remember magic
from a long time ago.

Take the still-burning cherry
from your joint and set it
like a glowing jewel in your chest.
Break skin.
Anyone's skin.

Eat a green blackberry.
Drink from the rainwater
pooled in a heavy red camellia.
Remember who you are.
Eat a Klonopin.

Walk down a street where you used to live.
Find your former home.
Who lives there now?
What kind of animal would they be?
What kind of animal are you?
Turn to the first tree you see.
Dig a burrow.
Sleep for many days.
Wake up.
Let your heart leap off
like a young rabbit.

Exhale until the stars
behind your eyes blink on.
With your eyes closed
to the earth but open
to the universe, move
toward the heat
of the breath
of any breathing thing.
Now your chest is empty.
Fill it with the just-washed light
of the wet new streets.

Chew the bark of the madrone.
Cinnamon, mushroom, wood smoke.
Don't spit it out.
Are you experiencing visions?
If no, spit it out.
Experience a vision.

Guess what
here is no living god
but something is moving
across the face of the waters.

Suddenly
everything has a name.

WHAT IS THE WAY TO ANYTHING

Space
I can't think of it
wide wild darkness
coiled in the ear like thought.
The haze of gorgeous sleep
but for like a billion years.

When it's all over it will be
the hungry sound of paper tearing.
Like sucking a penny.
Like going into the cold morning
with damp hair and sleep-creased skin.

When the heater clicks on
that is the exact temperature
of the universe, the exact scent
the toasted smell of dust.
Click click click.
I'm going to go ahead and
choose the next color of the cosmos.

In one galaxy it is five o'clock
in the evening on a Northeast November
and in another
I never have to be.

RITUAL FOR FINDING AND DESTROYING THE ROOT OF YOUR MANY MANY DEEP AND UNNAMEABLE SADNESSES

Make a list of all the things inside you.

Fur,
ink,
hay,
mud,
mist,
dust,
attic,
wool,
ashes,
steam,
ozone,
coffee,
smoke,
fir tree,
tea box,
sawdust,
lipstick,
cilantro,
pine sap,
gasoline,
whiskey,
camphor,
lavender,
wet lilac,
birch tar,
beeswax,
cat belly,
cut grass,
coca-cola,
salt spray,
old books,
cool moss,
junk shop,
new paint,
damp hair,

AS ABOVE   SO BELOW

sandpaper,
bathwater,
well water,
sprinklers,
eucalyptus,
shaded dirt,
clean sweat,
orange peel,
rising damp,
wet cement,
desert dusk,
crushed ant,
good honey,
import shop,
foxed edges,
boozy kisses,
incense ends,
sleeping skin,
warm amber,
face powder,
green shoots,
lime on knife,
rotting velvet,
dandelion sap,
dry driftwood,
burnt cigarette,
research rooms,
magnolia hearts,
wilting dianthus,
candy cigarettes,
new cedar fence,
empty cigar box,
spent matchstick,
behind your ears,
warped firewood,
sandalwood resin,
chlorinated water,
last day of school,
approaching snow,
fresh deck of cards,
blown-out matches,

AS ABOVE   SO BELOW

tannin-stained river,
my grandmother's house,
having been to the beach,
when the heater clicks on,
walking past the dry cleaner's,
rising angry from a late-evening nap,
tar under the boardwalk cooling in the night air,
window screen with the fist-sized hole furred with dust and moth wings,
the baked interior of a car parked for many hours at the path to the quieter beach,
4 o'clock in the afternoon on the last day of the last summer of never having to
be a child ever again.

Break
it up.

They are all inside you
because you put them there
or they were given to you
though you did not want them.

Gather them up.
Try not to remember.
You can't do it,
can you. Go to sleep.
Try again.

Force the form.
Find words or don't.
Vibrate inside
with a special kind
of scary not-being.
Vibrate inside with
a feeling like a sound
that will never stop,
so high and cold,
it burns and burns.

Force the form.
Take everyone
down with you.
Walk it out until

you realize there is no out,
just in, in, in in
in in. In in.
In. In.
In.
In.
In.

ST. AMBIEN

Why won't you help me
not feel like this, like
the watery January sun
on a day that never really started?
All the future pleasures smeared
across my cheek with the back
of my own terrible hand.

Almost winter every day.

I look for myself
in the patterns of moss
creeping over the low stone wall.
Abandoned train station.
That's right, I'll always be this way
a bowl of clouds in my stomach,
low green sky in my head.

It lives in my throat
and also everywhere else,
the burning need for nothing.
The bare wet branches
of the forsythia in November,
only for always. Can you imagine?
You can try.

I'm ok I'm ok I'm ok I'm ok
I'll be ok I'm ok I'm ok
is how to make other people feel
better about my feelings.
I'm just tired.

It starts like this:
Nothing feels good
lying in the stubbled grass
looking up at an airplane
wanting to be in that

place between places, never
having to be anywhere
never having to be.

It comes with things
it comes with poetry
with empathy which is the gift
of being set on fire many times a day
by other people's grief.
It comes with poetry.
Would I unknow it if I could?
I would unknow you if I could
you, this, it
everything about being
I would unknow.

It is absurd and unbeautiful.
There is no beauty
and there is no beauty because
everything is already dead.
Great flock of swans
Grazing in wet black fields.

Despair is a place you can never leave.
Everything you own is jetsam
left in the wake of
the great tide of grief.
I'm just being transparent.
My religion is basically poetry
which as we all know is death.

RITUAL FOR DISCOVERING WHY YOU FEEL SO BAD

Walk up the long hill.
Do not cry until I tell you you can cry.
Ok.
You can cry.
The sun rises later and later from its fulcrum of bruisy red.
Golden light for everyone but you
and all those windows beginning to warm in the early dark.
Don't let the beauty of the city comfort you.
Where the mountains meet the water meet the streets is not for you.
This dusting of snow won't last.
Winter will pull wet clouds over the smoky end of day.
Do you believe any of this?
No?
Go back to sleep alone and remember what I have told you
and remember the truth you made for yourself and no one else.

WINTER IS THE OLDEST SEASON

The eggs broke today
glass in the yolk, under my heel
I'm leaving
to be unfound.
To be unfound, a right removed
with marriage.

There is nowhere to go
but out.
Out in the soft morning
breath of the city breathes
my breath, ugly and sweet.
Watery sun
a balm for all the broken things.

Sunday
sad-colored and kind
to my sadness.
Everything is sleeping
under snowbanks.
That soft, warm winter grouse
those gentle feelings.

Little mosses pushing through the brick.
To be so small
and so soft
to make one's home in crumbling soft things.
To spore and spore
married to myself.

But aren't humans nice together?
Nice
on other humans late at night
in the mystery of dark and also light.
Triumph of triumph of sleep
and also in the not-sleeping.

I do my best sleeping in the car.

Mid-winter in the mountains
windows slowly fog
with memory.
It is true: without desire
there is no memory.
Without memory
there is no you.

Here, I made you this
coat of quietness and care.
Your sorrow is a door
you close and you lock.
My sorrow is a Sunday.

RITUAL FOR DISCOVERING WHETHER YOU CAN RECOVER FROM INDIFFERENCE

Say out loud: ok bye.

Board your sadness like a train.
Find your real name
scratched on the train window.
Remember this feeling.
The mystical nature of: not-being.
The mystical fuck-you of: disappearing.

You are right to imagine
I am not loveable.

Clap your hands.
Clap your hands.

Fill them with ocean.
Don't stop until I say you can.

Make a fist
now keep me in it.

Open the double doors of winter,
the new way in.
It's a new season I've invented just for you.
I have never physically been there.

Walk backwards until everything is ok again.
Everything has gone missing.
Everything is coming back.

Clap your hands.
Clap your hands.

Fill them with hair
cut grass
birch wands

poetry shit.
Yes.
Don't stop until everyone you know is dead.

Now bare your fangs
and see all my names reflected in your teeth.

PAIN AND WONDER

Driving, we pass
sparkles of midnight
in far-away towns.
It's a special quiet
in the nighttime car.
It's so good.

We are quiet
and cosmic.
We are sleepy
and alive.
Abandoned gas station
in a pool of yellow light.
Remember this feeling.

Repetition is a spell.
Headlights through fog
headlights through snow.
Rabbit leaping
through the beams.
Deer nosing
at the edge of the beams.

Remember this feeling
remember this feeling.

RITUAL FOR MOURNING WHILE THE DEAD WATCH

Put the urn on the counter.
Give it three dozen tuberoses bound
by rubber bands, crisscrossing
strings of gum pink and beige.
Shear the stems on a diagonal.
Does the urn like the flowers?
Find a tea light and let it burn.
Touch the greasy wax
with your fingertips
then peel it off as it dries.
Does the urn like music?
Play the urn some music.
Position the urn to the right
to the left
to the right
to the right no
to the right.
Stand barefoot at the counter
while you cry.
Remember all the times
you were unkind
to the urn.
No.
You can't actually do that.

THE BEGINNING OF POETRY

Have you been safe in the woods.
Have you been safe with the wolves.
Have you been safe in the treetops.
Are you safe in the fragrant pages.
Are you safe in my memory.
Have you been safe in the secret world of fear.
Have you been safe in the snow drifts.
Have you been safe in the folds of my dress.
Have you been safe in the kitchen in the dream.
Are you safe in the bed.
Have you ever been safe.
Do you think you will be safe in the city.
Do you think you will be safe in my quiet.
Were you safe inside me.
Are you going to be safe in the night park.
Are you safe inside history. No.

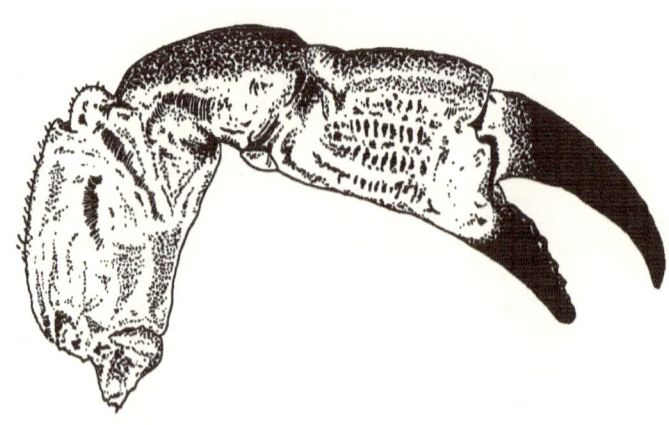

AS ABOVE　　　　　　　　　　　　　　　　SO BELOW

RITUAL FOR REVEALING THE SEVENTH SWORD

Pour a bag of cool pebbles on the table.
Find the one that tastes like beach.
How many secrets do you have?
Count the pebbles.
That many.
You have that many secrets.
Shake them out into the deep bowl of your belly.
Let a line of pumpkin spiders pick across your arm
while you lay out your cards
in the shape of what you used to be.
Keep the ocean to your left.
Are there 7 horns floating in the room?
Pick the smallest one and blow into it.
Do not turn over the next card.

SOUNDSOUND

Glass, bird, throat
wet finger on dry glass
holding shrieks in my loose fist
or dragging a hand through the ozone.
Get it out get it out get it out
I mean striking it
high in the ribs
really really hard.
Decay, sustain, release
like a fist, fast across
the face of morning.

Sound borne through matter like a wave
enclosed in the envelope
a signal received.
Transversing the unbearable medium
turbulence rings the moon like a bell.

Glass, bird, throat
terrific need to speak
open your mouth
and bees fly out
moving relative to the source,
oh adorable human,
keeping time
a bright ring
around a bright light
a new phase of moon
gone.

I could hear you calling
from the other mountain top
sweet diffraction
and the sound of something
coming from very far away
how a horse becomes
another horse just like that
and springs from your hand.

I touch you
and you bend
around my touch.

Loose light
spilled on dust
light gives a body
to the wire
sonorous body.
The wire sobs
hip-deep in salted ruin
under the scraping wave
the entire body participates
stranded under the power lines
magenta, cyan, black
oh adorable human
coiled, a fist
interacts with objects
sweet electric color, richness.
How a horse
becomes another horse.

Just like that
going the wrong way
electricity
I mean
striking it high
and tight in the ribs
get it out get it out get it out.

Fast across the face of morning
the city makes a noise like a bruise
diffraction cuts the prism
across the cheek.
The gentle echo
bends the transverse.
It's a way of being a color
two colors
or white and parchment
hip-deep on the crumpled canvas.
Decay, sustain, release.

where spiral is the threshold of hearing
and helix is the charge in the room
the threshold parts
a cloud
falling note
something to slide
along the wire.

Lilies
culvert culvert culvert
the throat of the afternoon
springs from your hand.
Lily, corridor, culvert.
The darkest
dark I have seen
and nimbus around
pistil and night and
ivory eating the charred morning.

There's a ghost
on the wire
lost voice, pleading
frequency on a naked chord
a noise like a bruise
and ghost moons
multiplying on the surface.

Dizzy elision
open your mouth
and bees fly out.
Helix, rarefaction
bright ring around bright
light source.

Through the wavering threshold
wet finger on dry glass
and the sound of
hands on hair.
Let them all watch
breathing from the table.
Slow rarefaction

                    up from the depths.

                         Sidereal day
                       terrible spectra
                    light makes saffron
              on the face of the waters.

                         Dizzy elision
                      pane under palm
                    and morning voices
                         snow on snow
                       snow impending
                      shadow of snow

                      smudged across
                  the face of the moon
                      which transmits
                       which receives
                        skin on paper
                 and signal perceived
                    over the low hills
                    foothills echoing.

        Sweetness, diffraction, sleep.
                Tattered banner, dirty
                       cut cut skyline
                   and the sound of
                        hands on hair
                     slip, catch, slip.
                        Terrific need
                             to speak
                       the sound of
                   something coming
                  from very far away.

           Generate, transmit, receive
                     terrifying aerial
                   I mean what is it
                they are dreaming of?
                        Every chord
                          in the world

at once
singing itself
to sleep.

Every chord
in the world at once
and gentle echo
tender unwanted sound
sonorous body body.

Some intervals seem
more beautiful than others.

Gold beams
wire dripping light
fast as fast as wings
inside the blinking lights they
are waiting for it, little filaments
frisson of bright white
or something that kills.

Oh gorgeous tangent
flickering outside
cumulous, blue
buzzing light
sweet electric objects.

And night passes
through matter
as a wave
and gentle echo

RITUAL FOR INVITING A CLOUD OF FIRE INTO A CLOSED ROOM

Turn off the light.
Darkness falls from the buildings.
Feel the not-there raise the down of your arms.
The dovecote in the yard is rustling.
A dusty brush of wing crosses your cheek.
The grounded dory lists to sweep the sky and
then you are ready at the cave's mouth in the cave's gentle breath.
Of course the cave isn't real.
Whatever disturbs the surface of thought
destroy it.
Feel the dip of wing, cold wind.
Can you feel my voice in your chest?
Count the gasps of your heart like a fish.
Listening is presence.
If you can remember touch
you can remember that crooked evening.
Set yarrow blazing
shake light loose from yarrow.
Let it fall for days from your hand.
Shout your honeyed fear into the night you are making.
You are an alleyway
you are secret passages
you are on fire.
Come in.
Repeat

I will see you through the curtain of my hair.
I will see you through the curtain of my hair.
I will see you through the curtain of my hair.

FUCKING TELL ME

There is a dove
there is a dove
there is a dove
there is a dove
there is a dove
there is a dove
it's scary time.
I am coming down your street.
I am coming for you
through gates of horn
through the window.
Tell me why
are spiders
why are spiders
drawn to water
at the actual end
of the actual world
you are standing there alone.

ACKNOWLEGEMENTS

ADULTHOOD, Sprung Formal, Spring 2018
RITUAL FOR BECOMING UNBORN, Heavy Feather Review, January 2020
RITUAL FOR BRINGING BACK THE DEAD, Heavy Feather Review, January 2020
RITUAL FOR CLEARING YOUR HEAD, Sprung Formal, Spring 2018
RITUAL FOR CONTINUING TO BE A WOMAN EVEN THOUGH YOU HAVE NEVER WANTED TO BE ANYTHING LESS THAN YOU WANT TO BE A WOMAN RIGHT NOW, Dream Pop Journal, Spring 2020
WHEN THERE IS NOWHERE ELSE TO GO, Fine Print, fall 2019

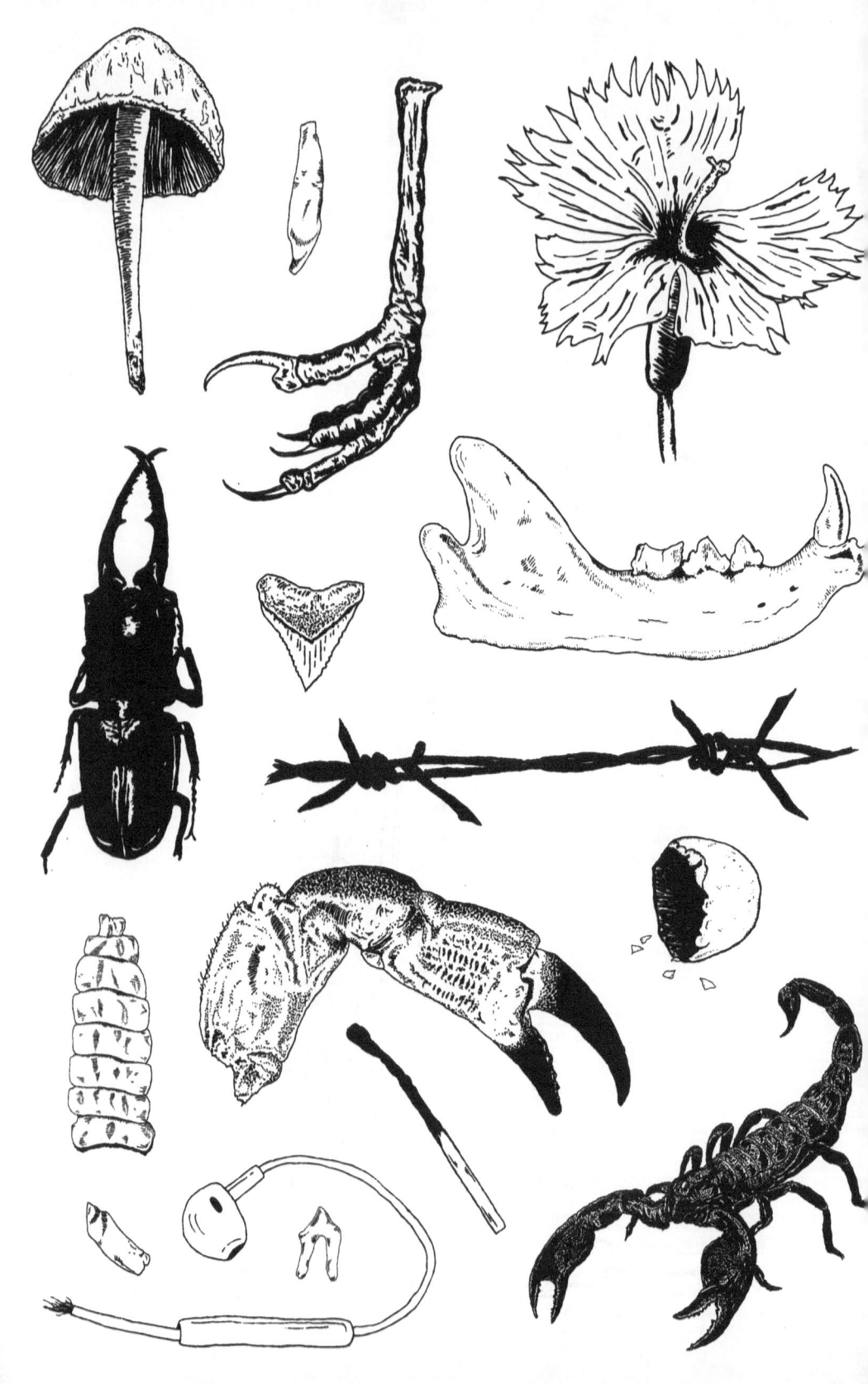